Hidden, Lost, and Discovered
UNDERGROUND
CITIES

Rourke
Educational Media

A Division of
Carson
Dellosa
Education

ESCAPE

Before Reading: *Building Background Knowledge and Vocabulary*

Building background knowledge can help children process new information and build upon what they already know. Before reading a book, it is important to tap into what children already know about the topic. This will help them develop their vocabulary and increase their reading comprehension.

Questions and Activities to Build Background Knowledge:

1. Look at the front cover of the book and read the title. What do you think this book will be about?
2. What do you already know about this topic?
3. Take a book walk and skim the pages. Look at the table of contents, photographs, captions, and bold words. Did these text features give you any information or predictions about what you will read in this book?

Vocabulary: *Vocabulary Is Key to Reading Comprehension*

Use the following directions to prompt a conversation about each word.

- Read the vocabulary words.
- What comes to mind when you see each word?
- What do you think each word means?

Vocabulary Words:
- attack
- bunkers
- invaders
- satellites
- stations
- tombs

During Reading: *Reading for Meaning and Understanding*

To achieve deep comprehension of a book, children are encouraged to use close reading strategies. During reading, it is important to have children stop and make connections. These connections result in deeper analysis and understanding of a book.

 Close Reading a Text

During reading, have children stop and talk about the following:

- Any confusing parts
- Any unknown words
- Text to text, text to self, text to world connections
- The main idea in each chapter or heading

Encourage children to use context clues to determine the meaning of any unknown words. These strategies will help children learn to analyze the text more thoroughly as they read.

When you are finished reading this book, turn to the next-to-last page for **After-Reading Questions** and an **Activity**.

Table of Contents

Hidden Cities

ARCTIC OCEAN

Montréal, Canada

EUR

NORTH
AMERICA

ATLANTIC
OCEAN

PACIFIC
OCEAN

AFRICA

SOUTH
AMERICA

ATLANTIC
OCEAN

SOUTHERN OCEAN

Can a city be a secret? It can if it is built underground. Underground cities are hiding all over the world. Let's explore!

Kaymaklı and Derinkuyu, Turkey

Beijing, China

Petra, Jordan

ASIA

PACIFIC OCEAN

INDIAN OCEAN

AUSTRALIA

ANTARCTICA

RÉSO

The city of Montréal, Canada has a secret. It's on top of an underground city called RÉSO!

Canada

Montréal

Lake Ontario

United States of America

Atlantic Ocean

RÉSO

STYLEXCHANGE

Winters in Canada are cold. People stay warm in RÉSO. Important places all over Montréal are connected through the underground city.

RÉSO

There's a lot to do in the underground city. You can find restaurants, shops, movie theaters, museums, metro **stations**, and more.

stations (STAY-shuhnz): places where tickets for trains or buses are sold and where passengers can get on and off

Petra

Petra, Jordan is a city built into mountains. The buildings were carved out of rock. It was built by a group of people called the Nabateans during the fourth century.

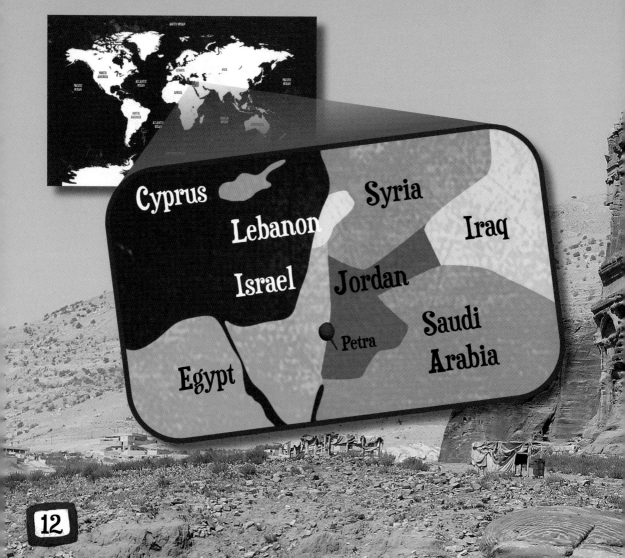

Cyprus

Syria

Lebanon

Iraq

Israel

Jordan

Petra

Saudi Arabia

Egypt

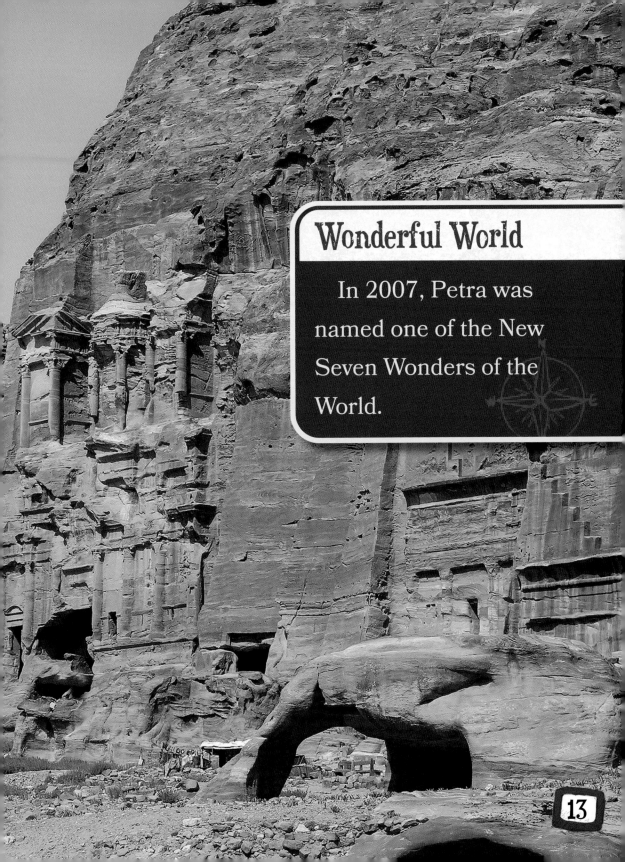

Wonderful World

In 2007, Petra was named one of the New Seven Wonders of the World.

Petra

It was hard to **attack** the city of Petra. When Petra became an important trading post, the Greek Empire got jealous. They tried to take over Petra. But the mountains surrounding Petra were a natural wall. The Nabateans used the mountains to keep the Greeks out.

attack (uh-TAK): to use violence against someone or something

Petra

Many of the biggest buildings in Petra are **tombs**. There also used to be theaters, gardens, houses, and a market.

tombs (tooms): rooms or buildings that hold dead bodies

Buried Secrets

Scientists used pictures from **satellites** and saw there is still a gigantic structure buried under the sand at Petra! What will be uncovered?

satellites (SAT-uh-lites): spacecraft that are sent into orbit around the Earth

Beijing's Underground City

Bunkers are created to keep people safe from the explosion of a bomb. They are built underground. During the Cold War, the city of Beijing, China built around 10,000 bunkers under the city.

China

Beijing

North Korea

South Korea

Yellow Sea

bunkers (BUHNG-kurz): underground
shelters, used especially during wartime

Beijing's Underground City

Entrances to the underground city are all over Beijing. Tunnels connect the bunkers. There were even plans for an underground skating rink and movie theater. Luckily, the bunkers were never needed.

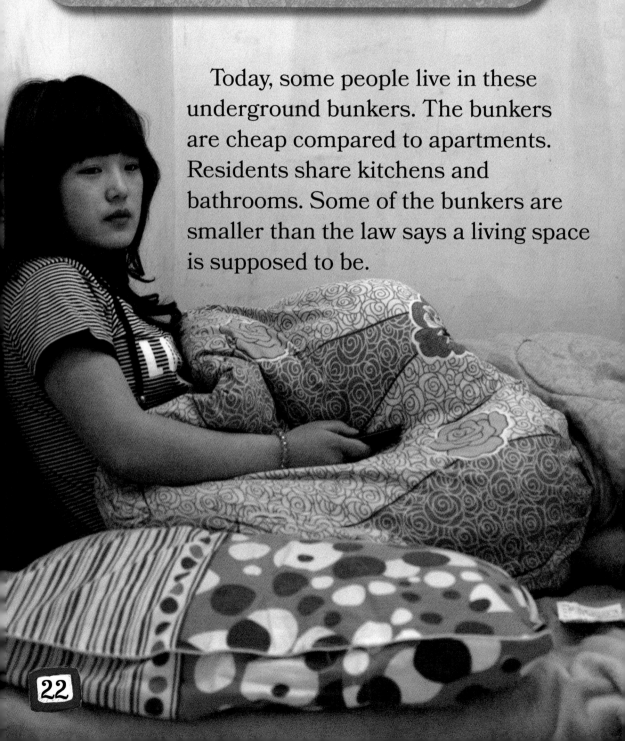

Beijing's Underground City

Today, some people live in these underground bunkers. The bunkers are cheap compared to apartments. Residents share kitchens and bathrooms. Some of the bunkers are smaller than the law says a living space is supposed to be.

23

Kaymaklı, Derinkuyu, & Beyond

The region of Cappadocia, Turkey is covered in volcanic rock. This rock is very soft. During the fourth century, the people of Cappadocia carved underground cities into the rock.

Artist's idea of what Derinkuyu looks like.

The underground cities are called Kaymaklı and Derinkuyu. The cities are made up of houses, churches, stables, tunnels, and storage areas. The people of Cappadocia were able to hide from **invaders** in these two cities.

invaders (in-VADE-urz): people who enter a place in large numbers to take control

Derinkuyu is the largest known underground city. It could hold 20,000 people. However, in 2013 a new underground city was accidentally discovered by construction workers. They were tearing down old houses when they found underground rooms and tunnels. Experts think this city will be even bigger than Derinkuyu.

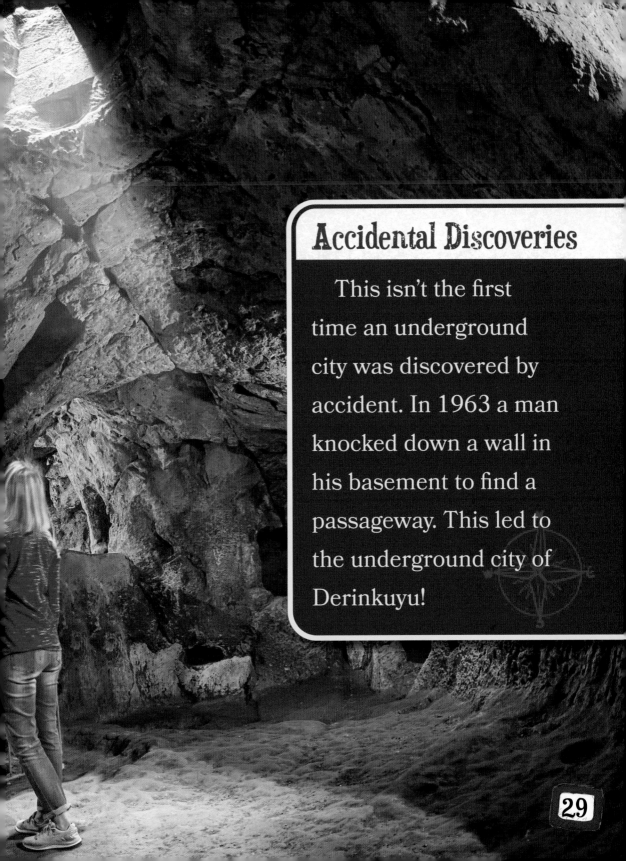

Accidental Discoveries

This isn't the first time an underground city was discovered by accident. In 1963 a man knocked down a wall in his basement to find a passageway. This led to the underground city of Derinkuyu!

Memory Game

Look at the pictures. What do you remember reading on the pages where each image appeared?

Index

After-Reading Questions

1. What is one reason a city might be built underground?

2. What would you find in the cities of Kaymaklı and Derinkuyu?

3. What are some of the largest buildings in Petra?

4. Why was it hard to attack Petra?

5. What are bunkers used for?

Activity

Imagine you are planning a trip to one of the underground cities. Which one would you most like to see? Why? Write a checklist of things you want to do and see while you are there.

About The Author

Hailey Scragg loves visiting and learning about new cities but she hasn't been to an underground city yet! She enjoys exploring her city of Columbus, Ohio with her husband and dog.

www.rourkeeducationalmedia.com

PHOTO CREDITS: Cover, page 1: ©Western Eyes Photography; pages 6-7: ©ventdusud; page 8, 9a, 9b: ©Design Pics / David Thompson/David Thompson/Newscom; page 10: ©Cindy Miller Hopkins / DanitaDelimont.com "Danita Delimont Photography"/ Newscom; page 10-11: ©Egmont Strigl imageBROKER/Newscom; page 11, 30: ©Design Pics / David Thompson/David Thompson/Newscom; page 12-13: ©vladj55; page 14, 30: ©sorincolac; page 15a: ©cinoby; page 15b: ©znm; page 16-17, 30: ©conceptualmotion; page 18-19: ©ynm_yn; page 20-21, 30: ©Cai Daizheng/UPPA/ZUMA Press/Newscom; page 22, 23: ©Sim Chi Yin/ Magnum Photos; page 24-25, 30: ©1001nights; page 26-27, 30: ©Dmytro Gilitukha; page 27: ©katesid; page 28-29: ©Natalia Moroz

Edited by: Madison Capitano
Cover design by: J.J. Giddings
Interior design by: J.J. Giddings

Library of Congress PCN Data

Underground Cities / Hailey Scragg
 (Hidden, Lost, and Discovered)
 ISBN 978-1-73164-330-8 (hard cover)
 ISBN 978-1-73164-294-3 (soft cover)
 ISBN 978-1-73164-362-9 (e-Book)
 ISBN 978-1-73164-394-0 (e-Pub)
Library of Congress Control Number: 2020945277

Rourke Educational Media
Printed in the United States of America
03-0902311937